Janice VanCleave's

Play and Find Out

about

Math

Easy Activities for Young Children

John Wiley & Sons, Inc.

New York • Chichester • Weinheim • Brisbane • Singapore • Toronto

Copyright © 1998 by Janice VanCleave
Illustrations copyright © 1997 by Michelle Nidenoff
Design and production by Navta Associates, Inc.

Published by John Wiley & Sons, Inc.
All rights reserved. Published simultaneously in Canada.

The publisher and author have made every reasonable effort to ensure that the experiments and activities in the book are safe when conducted as instructed but assume no responsibility for any damage caused or sustained while performing the experiments or activities in this book. Parents, guardians, and/or teachers should supervise young readers who undertake the experiments and activities in this book.

Library of Congress Cataloging-in-Publication Data

VanCleave, Janice Pratt.
    [Play and find out about math]
    Janice VanCleave's play and find out about math : easy activities for young children / Janice VanCleave.
        p.   cm.   — (Play and find out series)
    Includes index.
    ISBN 0-471-12937-2 (cloth : alk. paper).—ISBN 0-471-12938-0 (paper : alk. paper).
    1. Mathematics—Study and teaching (Primary) 2. Games in mathematical education.
I. Title. II. Series: VanCleave, Janice Pratt. Play and find out series.
QA135.5.V36   1997
372.7 044—dc21   96-53002

Printed in the United States of America
10 9 8 7 6 5 4 3 2

Dedication

This book is dedicated to Laura Fields Roberts, who is not only my colleague but a special friend. She and her kindergarten students field test each of my play and find out activities. What fun it is for me to read her review comments and see the pictures she sends of her adorable students performing the activities. There is only one Laura, but may the Lord bless me with more friends like her.

Acknowledgments

A special note of thanks to Andrew and Holly Black, Denise, William, Maria, and Anna Heimbigner, and Ron, Anne, Sarah, Benjamin, and Rebecca Skrabanek, who reviewed the activities and provided valuable comments I used to improve them.

I wish to express my appreciation to Donna Kelly Duncan, principal of St. Matthews Elementary School in Louisville, Kentucky. Because of Ms. Duncan's approval and support, the following students at St. Matthews, under the direction of Laura Roberts and her coworker Sandra Williams Petrey, tested the activities in this book: Tricia Baldwin, Brittany Ballinger, Amanda Boden, Antonio Brown, Stephanie Coy, Joshlyn Cross-Stone, Jovan Dawson, Courtney Duffey, Alexandra Foote, Kaitlin Goodhew, Chelsey Hallett, Jessica Hamilton, Dane Hardy, Taylor Hawkins, Emily Jimmerson, William Long, Amy Love, Saphire Miller, Taylor Mouser, David Presnell, Hannah Rapp, Kristin Shattuck, Beth Spurr, Sarah Thomas, and Orenzio Tobin.

Contents

A Letter from Janice VanCleave

Dear Friends,

Welcome to math playtime!

The play activities in this book are about math. Very young children may not know the words "fraction" or "volume," but give them a candy bar to share or a spoon and the makings for a peanut butter and jelly sandwich and watch their eyes light up!

Discovering things on their own gives kids a wonderful feeling of success. All they need are your friendly guidance, a few good ideas, and their natural curiosity. This book is full of fun ideas. It contains instructions for more than 50 simple, hands-on activities inspired by questions from real kids. While you play together, your child will find out the answers to questions such as "How can I do math on my fingers?" "Is my foot a foot long?" and lots of other things that children wonder about.

So get ready to enter into a math adventure.

Playfully yours,

Janice VanCleave

Before You Begin

 Read the activity completely before starting. When possible, practice doing the activity by yourself prior to your math play-time. This increases your understanding of the topic and makes you more familiar with the procedure and the materials. If you know the activity well, it will be easier for you to give instructions and answer questions. If you want to know more about the basic math behind the activity, see the Appendix.

 Select a place to work. The kitchen table is usually the best place for the activities. It provides space and access to an often-needed water supply.

3 **Choose a time.** There is no best time to play with your child, and play should be the main point when doing the activities in this book. Select a time when you will have the fewest distractions so that you can complete the activity. If your family has a schedule, you may allot a specific amount of time for the activity. You may want to set an exact starting time so the child can watch the clock and become more familiar with time. Try to schedule 5 to 10 minutes at the close of each session to have everyone clean up.

4 **Collect supplies.** You will have less frustration and more fun if all the materials are ready before you start. If food items are to be eaten, hands and supplies must be clean.

5 **Do not rush through the activity.** Follow each step carefully, and for sure and safe results, never skip steps or add your own. Safety is of the utmost importance, and it is good math technique to teach children to follow instructions when doing a math activity.

Tips on Materials

- Some activities call for water. If you want everything to be at the worktable, you can supply water in a pitcher or soda bottle.

- Extra paper towels are always handy for accidental spills, especially if the activity calls for liquids. A large bowl can be used for waste liquids, and the bowl can be emptied in the sink later.

- To save time, you can precut some of the materials (except string; see below).

- Do not cut string in advance, because it generally gets tangled and is difficult to separate. You and the child can measure and cut the string together.

- You may want to keep labeled shoe boxes filled with basic supplies that are used in many activities, such as scissors, tape, and marking pens.

- The specific sizes and types of containers listed in the material lists are those used when these activities were tested. This doesn't mean that substituting a different type of container will result in an experimental failure. Substitution of supplies should be a value judgment made after you read an activity to determine the use of the supplies. For example, you could replace an 8-inch (20-cm) circle of white paper with a round coffee filter that is equal, or nearly equal, to 8 inches (20 cm).

- For large groups, multiply the supplies by the number in the group so that each person can perform the activity individually. Some of the supplies (glue, for instance) can be shared, so read the procedure to determine this ahead of time.

6 **Have fun!** Don't worry if the child isn't "getting" the math principle, or if the results aren't exactly perfect. If you feel the results are too different from those described, reread the instructions and start over from step 1.

7 **Enjoy the wonder of participating in the learning process.** Remember, it is OK for your child not to discover the math explanation. For example, when you perform the activity "Reversed," the child may be too excited to stop making butterflies and listen to your explanation about symmetry. Don't force the child to listen. Join in the fun and make a magic moment to remember. Later, when questions about symmetry arise, you can remind the child of the fun time that you had making butterflies with matching wings, then repeat the activity, providing the explanation.

Counting

Petals

Round Up These Things

dark marking pen
flower with 5 petals
(such as a violet)
flower with 6 petals
(such as a lily)

I wonder . . . How many petals do flowers have?

Let's find out!

Later You'll Need

scissors
rectangular dishwashing
  sponge
tap water
tempera paint: red and
  yellow
2 paper plates
sheet of white paper
crayons

❶ Use the marking pen to place a dot on one petal of the flower with five petals.

❷ Starting with the petal that has the dot on it, count all the petals. Touch each petal with your pointer finger as you count it.

❸ Stop counting when you get to the petal with the dot. Do not count the petal with the dot again.

❹ Repeat steps 1 to 3 with the second flower.

So Now We Know

One flower has five petals, and the other has six petals. Different types of flowers have different numbers of petals.

More Fun Things to Know and Do

Make a picture of a flower that has eight petals.

- **ADULT STEP** Cut the sponge in half. Cut a circle from one half and a petal shape from the other half.

- Moisten the sponge cutouts with water, and squeeze out the excess water.

- Pour a little paint in each plate.

- Dip the round sponge in the yellow paint, then press it against the paper. Place the yellow circle just above the center of the paper.

- Make a petal by dipping the petal-shaped sponge in the red paint and pressing it against the paper above the yellow circle. Make another petal below the yellow circle.

- Make two more petals, one on either side of the yellow circle.

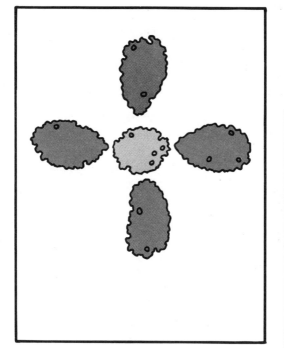

- Add four more petals by placing a petal between each pair of the first four petals.

- Use the crayons to add a stem and leaves to the flower.

How Many?

I wonder ...
How much is a dozen?

Let's find out!

Round Up These Things

empty 1-dozen egg carton

Later You'll Need

the same egg carton
        plus
pencil
ruler
sheet of typing paper
scissors
12 small plastic figures,
   such as dinosaurs, that
   fit inside the egg carton
   cups

1 Open the egg carton and place it on a table.

2 Using your finger, touch and count each egg cup in the egg carton.

So Now We Know

The egg carton holds one dozen eggs. You counted 12 egg cups, one for each egg. This means that one dozen eggs is equal to 12 eggs. Anytime you count out 12 things, you are counting out one dozen things.

More Fun Things to Know and Do

1 Use the egg carton to practice counting and writing the numbers from 1 to 12.

- Draw twelve 2-inch (5-cm) squares on the paper.

- Cut out the squares.

- Write the numbers 1 through 12 on the squares.

- Say "one" as you place square 1 in the first egg cup in the egg carton.

- Say "two" as you place square 2 in the second egg cup.

- Continue placing the numbers in order in the egg cups, saying each number as you place it.

2 Use the egg carton to count out one dozen dinosaurs.

- Place a plastic dinosaur in each egg cup.

- Count the dinosaurs as you place them in the egg cups.

Numbers

Finger Math

1 Look at the illustration and practice holding the fingers of your left hand in the position shown for each of the numbers. Lift your fingers one at a time to count from 1 to 5.

2 Now you are ready to use the fingers of your other hand. Practice holding your fingers in the position shown for each of these numbers. Lift your fingers one at a time to count from 6 to 10.

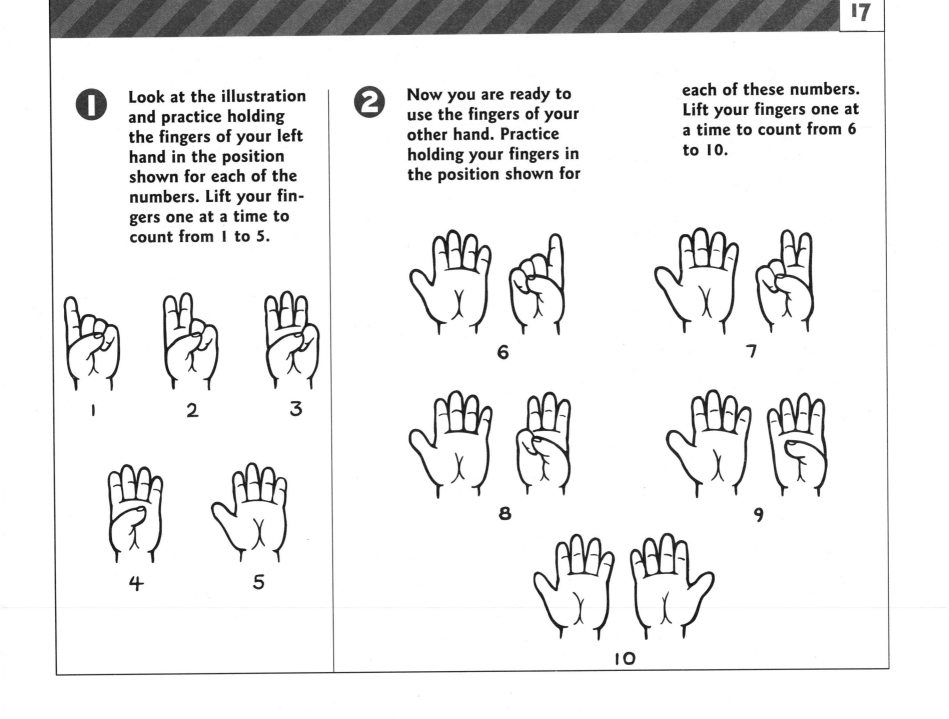

1   2   3

4   5

6   7

8   9

10

3 Now use the fingers of your two hands to add numbers of 5 or less. For example, to answer "How much is two plus three?" hold up two fingers on one hand and three fingers on the other hand.

4 Count the number of fingers you are holding up on both hands. The answer will be five.

5

So Now We Know

You are able to count and add up to ten on your ten fingers.

More Fun Things to Know and Do

You can also use your fingers to subtract numbers of 10 or less. If you are asked, "How much is five minus two?" do this to find the answer.

- Hold up five fingers.

5

- Then bend two fingers down.

3

- Count the number of fingers you are holding up. The answer will be three.

Dinosaur Math

I wonder . . . How can I use my toys to do math?

1 2 3 4 5
3 - 2 =

Let's find out!

Round Up These Things

cereal bowl
7 small plastic dinosaur
   figures (or other figures)

Later You'll Need

the same materials
        plus
2 more cereal bowls

Place the bowl and dinosaurs on a table.

 To answer the question "How much is six minus two?" count out 6 dinosaurs and place them in the bowl.

 Remove 2 of the dinosaurs from the bowl and place them on the table.

 Count the number of dinosaurs left in the bowl.

So Now We Know

The word minus means to take away. You had 6 dinosaurs in the bowl and took away 2. There were 4 dinosaurs left in the bowl. So the answer is 6 – 2 = 4.

More Fun Things to Know and Do

You can use the dinosaur figures to add. Here's how to answer " How much is four plus three?"

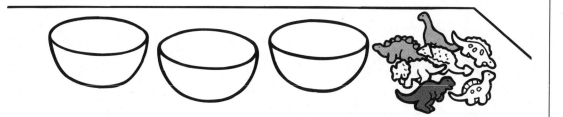

- Place the 3 bowls next to each other on the table.

- Count out 4 dinosaurs and place them in the first bowl.

- Count out 3 dinosaurs and place them in the second bowl.

- Hold the first bowl in your hands.

- Say "four" as you pour the 4 dinosaurs into the third bowl.

- Hold the second bowl in your hands and say "plus three," then pour the 3 dinosaurs into the third bowl.

- Count the dinosaurs in the third bowl.

- The answer is 4 + 3 = 7.

Just Alike

Round Up These Things

roll of cookie dough (Rolls without nuts or chocolate chips work best.)
cutting board
sharp knife
 (to be used only by an adult)
ruler
cookie sheet
toothpick
dinner knife or plastic knife

Later You'll Need

can of soda
2 identical clear drinking glasses
oven mitts
NOTE: This experiment requires an oven.

1 ADULT STEP Place the dough on the cutting board, and cut 2 slices of dough about ½ inch (1.25 cm) thick.

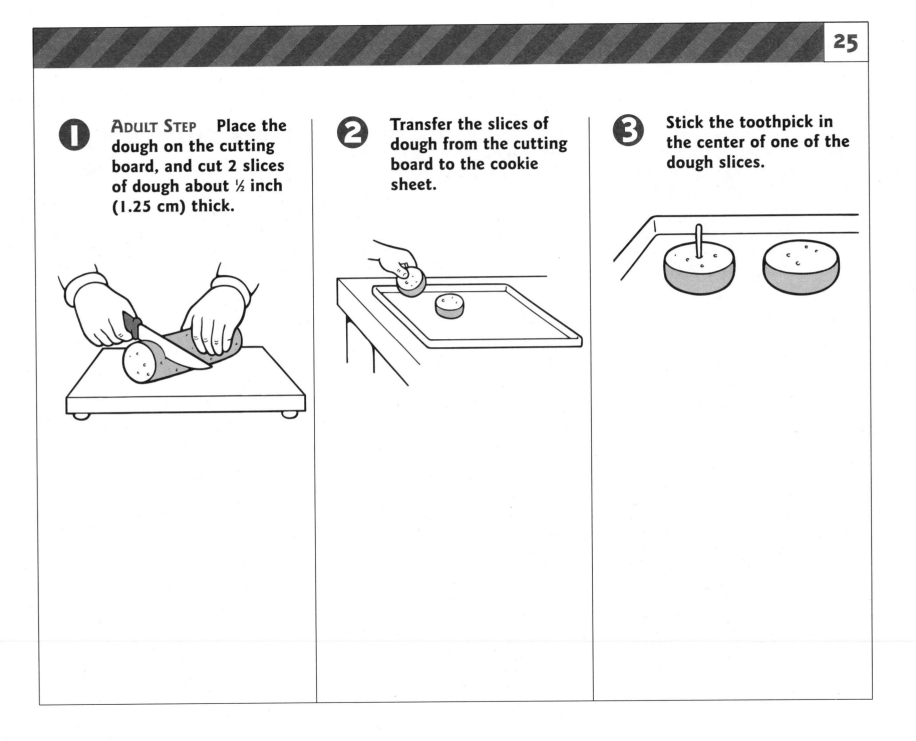

2 Transfer the slices of dough from the cutting board to the cookie sheet.

3 Stick the toothpick in the center of one of the dough slices.

Hold the dinner knife so that its edge is next to the toothpick and across the slice of dough. Push the knife down and move it back and forth to cut through the dough.

 Look at the sizes of the 2 pieces of dough that are formed, and compare them to the size of the uncut dough slice.

 Repeat steps 1 through 4 using the remainder of the dough.

So Now We Know

Cutting across the center of the dough slice produced 2 pieces of about the same size. Each of the smaller pieces is one-half (½) as big as the whole slice of dough.

More Fun Things to Know and Do

1 Baking changes the shape of dough. Here's how to bake the dough pieces and discover how they change:

- Remove the tooth-pick.

- ADULT STEP Bake the cookie slices according to the directions on the package.

- ADULT STEP Use the oven mitts to remove the cookies from the oven. Set them aside to cool.

- After the cookies have cooled, compare the changes in Shape. The cookies will be fatter, but the cut slices will still be smaller than the uncut slices.

2 A can of soda can be divided in half by pouring equal amounts into 2 identical glasses.

- Pour part of the soda into one glass and the rest into the second glass.

- Stand the glasses side by side and compare the level of the soda in each. If the soda in one glass is higher than in the other, pour soda from the glass

that has more soda into the glass that has less soda. Keep pouring the soda back and forth until their levels look equal.

- You now have one-half a can of soda in each glass.

Divided

I wonder . . . How can I share my candy bar with friends?

Let's find out!

Round Up These Things

bar of chocolate candy (Soft candy
  without nuts works best.)
saucer or paper plate
3 helpers

Later You'll Need

bar of soft chocolate candy without nuts
cutting board
adding-machine paper
pen
scissors
dinner knife
*NOTE: If your hands and supplies are kept
  clean, the candy in the following experiments can be eaten.*

1 Remove the paper wrapper from the candy bar.

 2 Hold the candy bar in both hands so that your thumbs touch in the center of the bar.

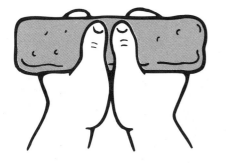

3 Break the candy bar in half by pressing with your thumbs. Each piece of candy is about one-half (½) of the candy bar.

4 Lay one of the candy halves on the saucer.

5 Hold the other half of the candy in your hands and break it in half. Place these 2 smaller pieces of candy in the saucer.

6 Repeat step 5 using the other half of the candy bar. Now you have 4 smaller pieces of candy. Each piece of candy is about one-fourth (¼) of the candy bar.

7 Lay the candy pieces side by side in the saucer. If the candy is equally divided into 4 pieces, the pieces will be the same length. How good were you at guessing where to break the candy?

8 Share your candy bar with three friends.

So Now We Know

By splitting the candy bar in half, then in half again, you were able to make 4 nearly equal pieces.

More Fun Things to Know and Do

Here's a more accurate way to divide a candy bar into 4 equal pieces.

- Remove the wrapper from the candy bar and place the bar on the cutting board.

- Lay the adding-machine paper next to the candy bar so that one end of the candy bar lines up with one end of the paper. Mark the other end of the paper where it lines up with the other end of the candy bar.

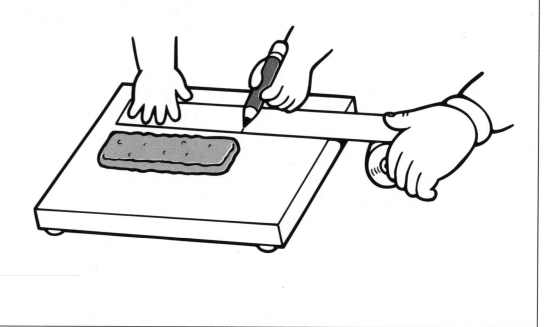

- Cut the paper on the mark.

- Fold the paper in half twice in the same direction and then unfold it.

- Lay the paper on the cutting board and set the candy bar on the paper so that the ends line up.

Leave enough of the paper sticking out along the side to see the folds in the paper.

- With the dinner knife, make four grooves in the candy bar to line up with the four folds in the paper.

- ADULT STEP   Slice the candy bar at each of the grooves.

- Lay the candy pieces side by side and decide if the pieces are of equal size.

Time

Ticktock

Round Up These Things

clock or watch with a second hand that stops with each second

I wonder . . . How long is five seconds?

Later You'll Need

pencil
sheet of typing paper

Let's find out!

1 Look at the clock and find the three hands.

2 Locate the hand that is thinner and faster moving than the other two hands. This is called the second hand.

3 Watch the second hand until it points to a number, such as the number 12. Then, count how many times the second hand moves before it points to the next number on the clock, such as the number 1.

4 Repeat step 3, with the second hand pointing to another number. Count the seconds before the hand reaches the next number.

SECOND HAND

So Now We Know

Every time the second hand on the watch or clock moved, 1 second of time passed. Starting at number 12, or any number on the clock, the second hand moved five times before reaching the next number. That means it took 5 seconds for the second hand to move from one number to the next.

More Fun Things to Know and Do

It takes 1 minute for the second hand to make one complete turn around a clock's face. Since it takes 5 seconds for the second hand to move from one number to the next, you can count by 5s to discover how many seconds are in 1 minute.

- Draw the face of a clock on the paper.

- Count by 5s as you touch each number. Pointing to the number 1, say "five." Pointing to the number 2, say "ten," and so on. Continue until you touch the number 12. You should have counted to the number 60. A minute has 60 seconds in it.

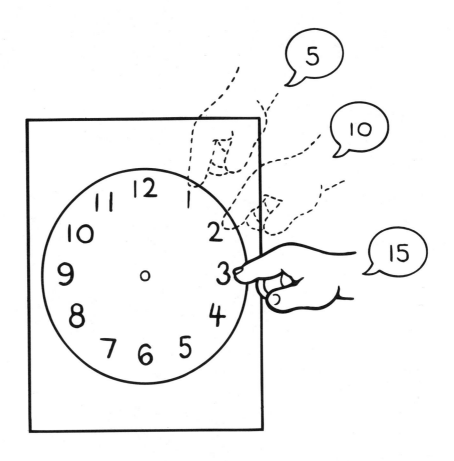

Day by Day

I wonder . . . How many days are in each month?

Let's find out!

Round Up These Things

your hands

Later You'll Need

sheet of typing paper
ruler
pen
photocopier
calendar
colored markers

1 Make a fist with your left hand. Look at the back of your left hand. You will see that your knuckles stick up and that there are valleys between them.

2 With the pointer finger of your right hand, touch the knuckle of the little finger of your left hand. At the same time, say the name of the first month of the year, January.

3 Move your finger from the knuckle to the valley and say the name of the second month of the year, February.

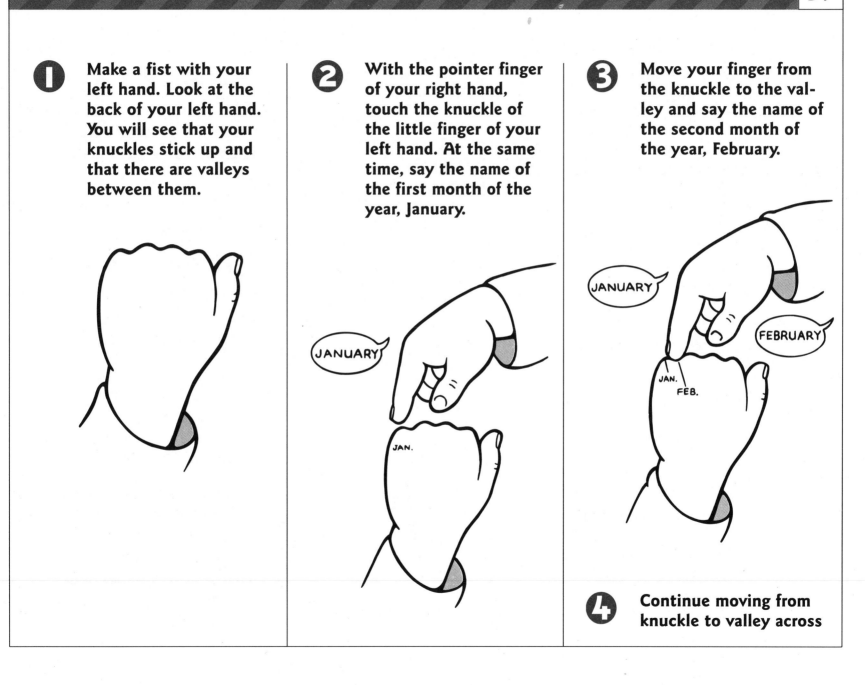

4 Continue moving from knuckle to valley across

the fist of your left hand, naming the months.

 After touching the knuckle of your left pointer finger for July, make a fist with your right hand. Use your left hand to point to the knuckle of your right pointer finger and say "August." Continue moving across your

right fist until you get to December.

 Look at the diagram. The months with 31 days are on the knuckles, and the months with 30 days are in the valleys. (The exception is February, which only has 28 days, or 29 days in a leap year. A leap year has 366 days, and other years have 365 days.)

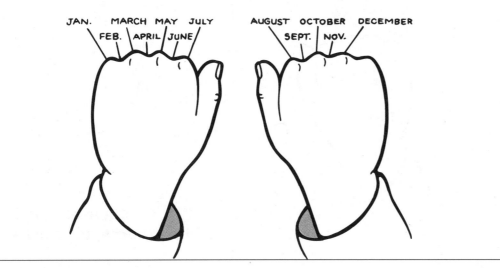

JAN.   MARCH MAY JULY
FEB. APRIL JUNE

AUGUST OCTOBER DECEMBER
SEPT. NOV.

So Now We Know

With this system, you always have an easy way to figure out how many days are in each month.

More Fun Things to Know and Do

Now that you know the number of days for each month, you can make a calendar.

- Fold the sheet of typing paper in half three times in the same direction. Unfold the paper.

- Refold the same piece of paper in the opposite direction three times in the same direction. Unfold the paper. The paper is divided into 64 rectangles.

- Use the ruler and pen to draw lines over the fold lines. Draw lines only around 7 rectangles across and 7 rectangles down. Leave space at the top for the month's name and space on the side to color your own pictures to represent each month.

- Write the days of the week in the top row of rectangles. You now have a calendar master.

Sun.	Mon.	Tues.	Wed.	Thur.	Fri.	Sat.

- Use a photocopier to make 12 copies of your calendar master. Save your original to use another year.

- Write the name of a month on the top of each page.

- Fill in the rectangles with the numbers for the days of each month. Look at a calendar for December of the previous year to figure out the day when January starts. Use the counting system you just learned to figure out the number of days in each month. Remember to start each month on the day after the last day of the month before.

- Using a colored marker, add pictures. Flying a kite represents the windy month of March.

March

Sun.	Mon.	Tues.	Wed.	Thur.	Fri.	Sat.
						1
2	3	4	5	6	7	8
9	10	11	12	13	14	15
16	17	18	19	20	21	22
23	24	25	26	27	28	29
30	31					

Shapes

Around and Around

Round Up These Things

one-hole paper punch
1-by-6-inch (1.25-by-15-cm) strip of thin card-board (such as from the back of a writing tablet)
poster board
2 pencils

Later You'll Need

different size lids and caps from jars and bottles
sheet of typing paper
pencil

1 Use the paper punch to make two holes in the cardboard strip, one at each end.

2 Lay the cardboard strip in the center of the poster board.

3 Stand one pencil on its point in one of the holes in the cardboard strip.

4 Stand the second pencil on its point in the second hole in the cardboard strip.

5 Keeping the second pencil in place, move the other pencil around, with its point pressed against the paper, until you have drawn a complete circle.

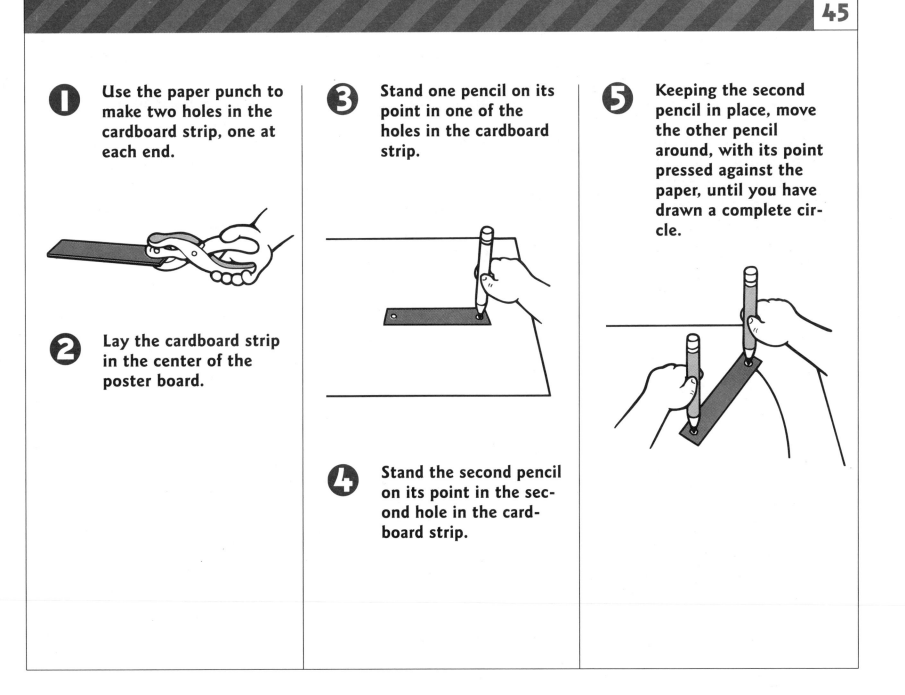

So Now We Know

A circle is a curved line drawn around a center point. The center point of your circle is the point where the still pencil touched the paper. The cardboard kept the drawing pencil the same distance from the center point all the way around the circle.

More Fun Things to Know and Do

Many things are shaped like a circle, such as bicycle wheels, rings, and lids on jars. You can also draw a circle by tracing around a round object. Here's how you can draw a bear using only circles.

- Place a large lid on the paper.

- Hold the lid in place with one hand while you trace around the lid with the pencil. This circle forms the body of the bear.

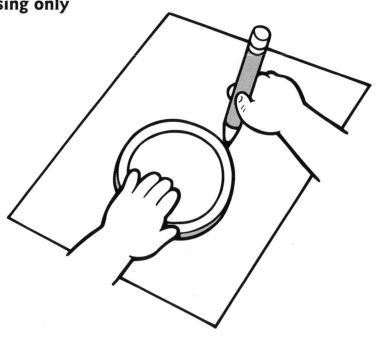

- Place a smaller lid at the top of the large circle, and trace around the lid. This circle forms the head of the bear.

- Use different size lids and caps to make other circles that complete a bear design like the one shown.

Magic or Math?

Round Up These Things

pencil
ruler
sheet of typing paper
scissors
dime
quarter

Later You'll Need

the same materials
        except
dime and quarter
        plus
string
ruler

I wonder . . . How can I do a math trick?

Let's find out!

① Use the ruler to draw a 3-by-3-inch (7.5-by-7.5-cm) square on the paper.

② Cut out the square.

③ Fold the square in half and lay it on the table.

④ Place the dime on the center of the fold so that the coin is half on the paper.

⑤ Use the pencil to trace around the half of the coin on the paper.

⑥ Remove the coin.

⑦ ADULT STEP Cut out the half circle drawn on the paper, cutting through both layers of paper.

⑧ Drop the quarter inside the folded paper so that it pokes through the hole cut in the paper. The quarter is too large to fall through the small hole.

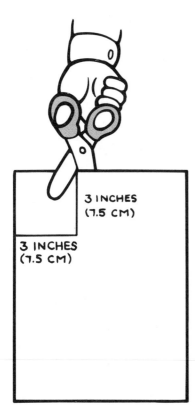

3 INCHES (7.5 CM)

3 INCHES (7.5 CM)

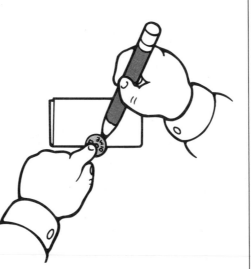

Hold the bottom corners of the paper between your thumbs and pointer fingers.

10 Gently, without tearing the paper, pull the paper so that the hole is slightly stretched. Bring the top corners of the paper together. The coin will drop "magically" through the hole in the paper.

11 After you have practiced the trick, try it in front of an audience. Announce that you can push a quarter through a dime-size hole. You might say a magic word, such as "abracadabra," just before bringing the corners of the paper together.

So Now We Know

The quarter did not magically fall through the hole. The magic words were just for fun. What really happened was that stretching and bending the paper changed the hole from a ring shape called a circle to an egglike shape called an oval. The oval is wider than the circle, so the quarter fell through the stretched hole. The size of the hole stayed the same; only its shape changed.

More Fun Things to Know and Do

Here's a way to see how changing a shape from a circle to an oval makes it wider.

- Cut a 12-inch (30-cm) piece of string.

- Tie the ends of the string together, and lay the string in the center of the paper.

- Arrange the string in the shape of a circle. On the paper, make marks with the pencil on the left and right sides of the circle.

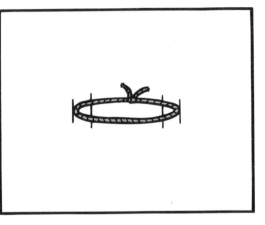

- Now, shape the string into an oval by pulling out on the left and right sides of the string. Make marks with the pencil on the left and right sides of the oval.

- Measure the distance between the first two pencil marks and the second two pencil marks. Notice how much wider the oval is than the circle.

Three Sided

Round Up These Things

ruler
4-by-8-inch (10-by-20-cm)
 piece of light-colored paper
sharpened pencil
scissors
transparent tape
unsharpened pencil
colored markers

Later You'll Need

tracing paper
colored marker
scissors
glossy, color magazine pages
 that can be cut into pieces
unsharpened pencil
glue stick
24-inch (60-cm) piece of colored yarn

1 Lay the ruler across the paper near one short end. Make a mark in the center of the paper, 2 inches (5 cm) from the long ends.

2 Lay the ruler across the paper from the mark to a corner at the opposite end of the paper. Draw a line on the paper from the mark to the corner.

3 Repeat step 2, moving the ruler to the opposite corner.

4 Cut along the lines you just drew.

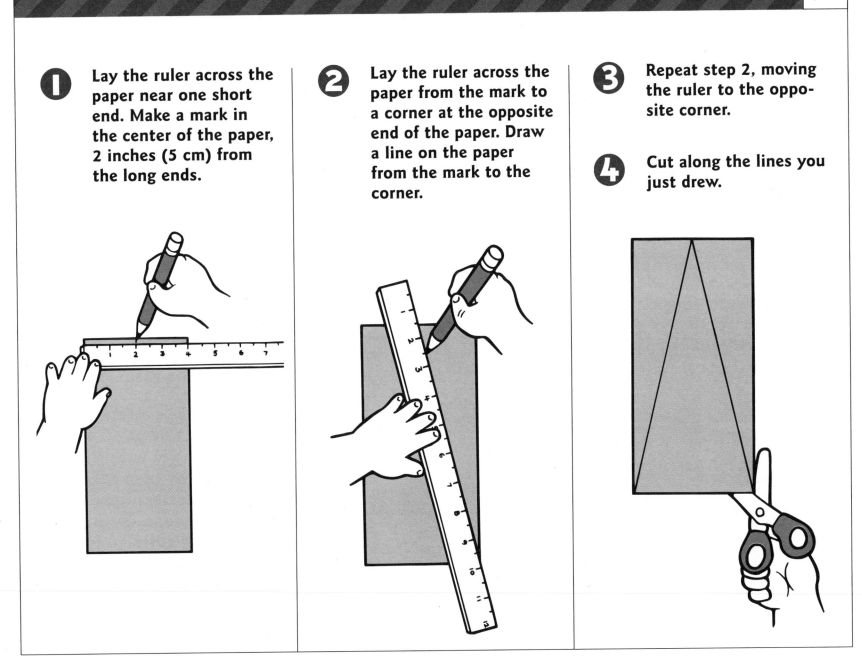

Keep the center piece of paper and throw away the other pieces.

 Tape the short side of the paper to the unsharpened pencil.

 Use the markers to draw a picture and write a celebration message, such as HAPPY BIRTHDAY, on the paper.

So Now We Know

A banner is a flag with special words on it. Banners come in all shapes and sizes. The banner you made has three sides. A three-sided shape is called a triangle.

More Fun Things to Know and Do

 You can make a bead necklace out of rolled paper triangles.

- Lay the tracing paper over the triangle pattern on page 55.

- Use the colored marker to trace the pattern on the paper. Then, cut out the pattern.

- Lay the pattern on the magazine page, draw around it with the marker, then cut out the design. Repeat this procedure, cutting a triangle design for each bead you wish to make.

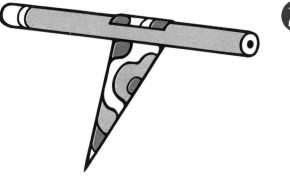

Triangle
Bead
Pattern

2 Determine how the width of the triangle design changes the size of the bead by making beads with different size triangles from the magazine pages.

pointed end. Hold the end firmly for a few seconds to allow the glue to set.

- Slip the bead off the pencil, and make more beads the same way.

- When you have enough beads, thread them on the yarn and tie a knot in the ends. Your necklace of rolled triangle beads is ready to wear.

- Place the short side of one triangle over the pencil and wrap it around the pencil.

- When you reach the pointed end of the triangle, put a dot of glue under the

Holders

Let's find out!

I wonder . . . How can I make a box?

Round Up These Things

sheet of typing paper
pencil
scissors
glue stick

Later You'll Need

sheet of typing paper
scissors

TOYS

1 Lay the paper over the box pattern.

2 Carefully trace the pattern on the paper, including all the labels and dashed lines.

3 Cut the pattern out of the paper along the solid lines.

Fold the paper along the dashed lines, making all folds in the same direction.

 Fold the paper so that the tabs fit over their corresponding sides—tab A over side A, tab B over side B, and so on.

 Use the glue to secure the tabs to the sides.

So Now We Know

You have made an open box. A box is a container for holding or carrying things. It has four rectangular sides and a rectangular bottom.

More Fun Things to Know and Do

Here's how to make a cup from paper.

- Fold one corner of the paper toward the opposite side to form a triangle.

- Cut off the strip of paper that is left over.

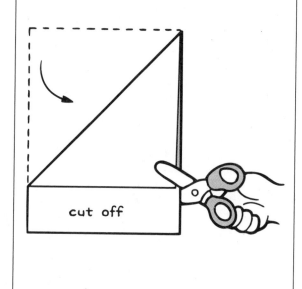

cut off

- Turn your triangle so that the fold is at the bottom.

- Fold corner A to touch point E, the center of the right side.

- Fold corner F to touch point B, the center of the left side.

- Open the cup and fill it with anything you like. Your cup can even be filled with water if you need a drink.

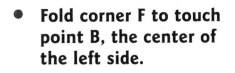

- Fold corner C forward and corner D backward.

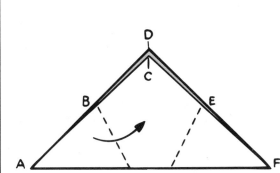

From the Heart

I wonder . . . How can I make a valentine?

BE MINE

Let's find out!

Round Up These Things

4-inch (10-cm) square piece of red construction paper
pencil
scissors
sheet of typing paper
glue stick

Later You'll Need

8-inch (20-cm) square of construction paper (bright color)
pencil
scissors

1 Fold the red paper in half.

2 Draw half of a heart on the folded edge of the paper.

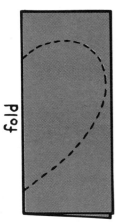

fold

3 ADULT STEP Cut out the heart shape along the line drawn.

4 Keep the shape cut from the paper and discard the rest of the paper. (The wastepaper can be kept for other projects.)

5 Open the folded shape. You have made a heart.

6 Make a valentine by folding the typing paper in half twice as shown. Glue the heart to the front of the folded paper.

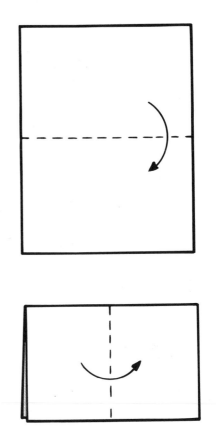

7 Write a valentine message such as the one shown.

So Now We Know

When some shapes, such as a heart, are folded in half, the two halves match each other exactly.

More Fun Things to Know and Do

Some shapes have patterns that match each other exactly when folded in two or more directions instead of just one. Here's how to make a paper flower that has matching parts.

- Fold the paper in half twice as in step 6 of the original experiment.

- Draw the dashed line on the folded paper as shown.

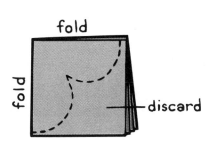

- **ADULT STEP** Cut along the dashed line. Discard the part indicated. (The wastepaper can be kept for other projects.)

- Unfold the paper.

- Fold the flower shape in half along one of the fold lines. Observe how the two halves fit.

- Unfold the paper and refold along the other fold line. Again, observe how the two halves fit.

- Can you think of another way to fold the paper so that a different pattern is seen fitting together?

Reversed

Round Up These Things

sheet of typing paper
scissors
poster paint: any color
4-inch (10-cm) square of
  black construction
  paper
ruler
glue stick
black marker

Later You'll Need

soft-leaded pencil
sheet of typing paper
lemon-size piece of modeling clay
rectangular hand mirror

1 Fold the paper in half twice.

2 Unfold the paper and cut along the fold lines. You will have 4 smaller pieces of paper.

3 Fold one of the small pieces of paper in half by placing the long sides together.

4 Unfold the paper partway and place two pea-size blobs of paint about ½ inch (1.25 cm) apart in the center of the fold.

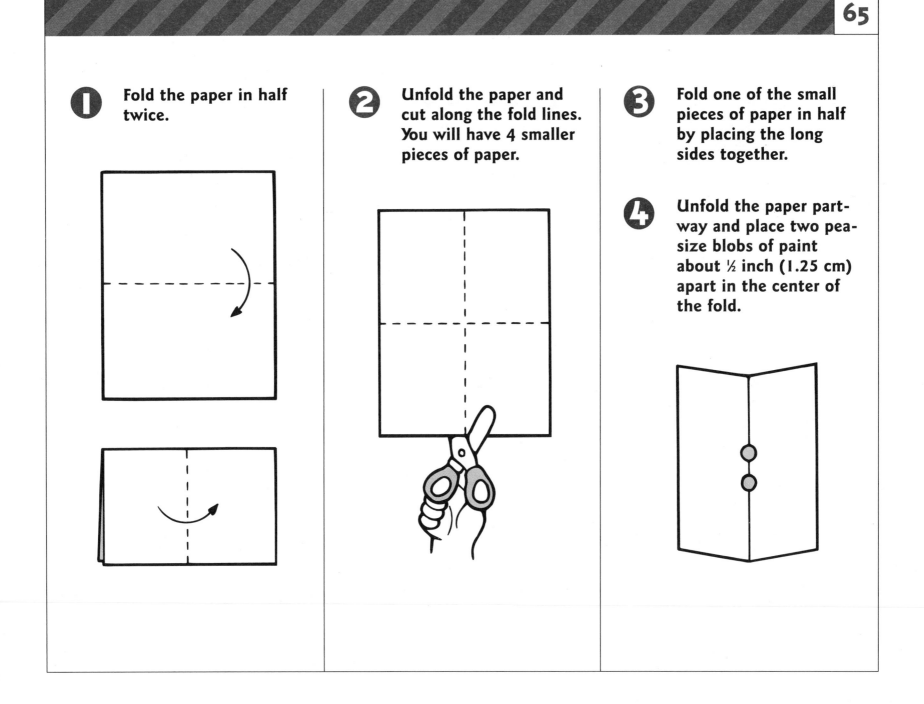

5 Fold the paper, and use your fingers to spread the paint by pressing and rubbing the paper in two directions as shown.

6 Unfold the paper and allow the paint to dry.

7 Cut a 1-by-4-inch (1.25-by-10-cm) body for the butterfly from the black paper. Shape the ends of the body as shown.

8 Glue the body to the center of the paint blot.

9 Use the marker to add antennae to the top of the body.

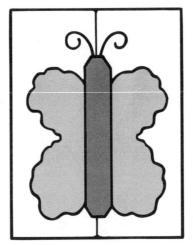

10 Repeat steps 3 through 9 to make butterfly designs on the 3 remaining pieces of paper.

So Now We Know

The shape of the paint blot is the same on both sides of the fold line. Like the wings of real butterflies, the wings formed by the paint are mirror images of each other.

More Fun Things to Know and Do

Have you ever tried to write your name backward? Here's an easy way to do it.

- With the pencil, write your name on the paper. Press down hard so that the letters are very dark.

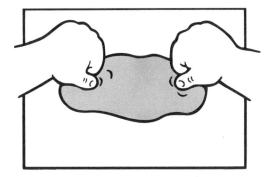

- Hold the mirror next to the clay at the end of your backward name and read the mirror image of your writing.

- Turn the clay over by lifting its right edge. Your name will be printed backward on the clay.

- Use your thumbs to press the clay against the paper where your name is written.

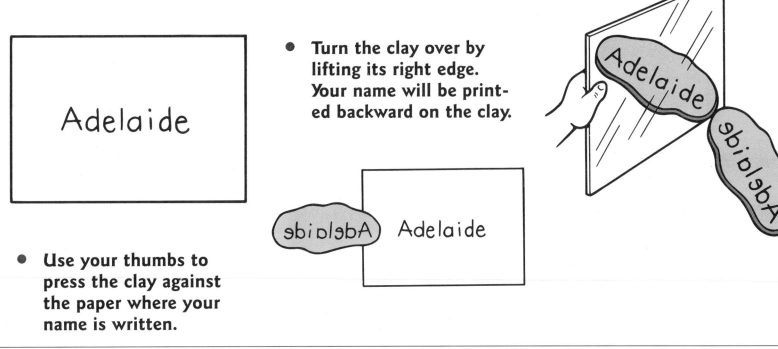

Star Designs

I wonder . . . How can I draw a star?

Let's find out!

Round Up These Things

tracing paper or light-
  weight typing paper
pen

Later You'll Need

cutting board
knife (to be used only by an adult)
apple
drinking straw
24-inch (60-cm) piece of yarn

MARKERS

1 Place the paper over the dot pattern.

2 Starting at dot 1, draw a straight line to dot 2, then draw a straight line to dot 3.

3 Continue following the numbers to connect the dots with straight lines. Some of the lines will cross.

4 ADULT STEP Cut out the star, and fold it carefully down the middle.

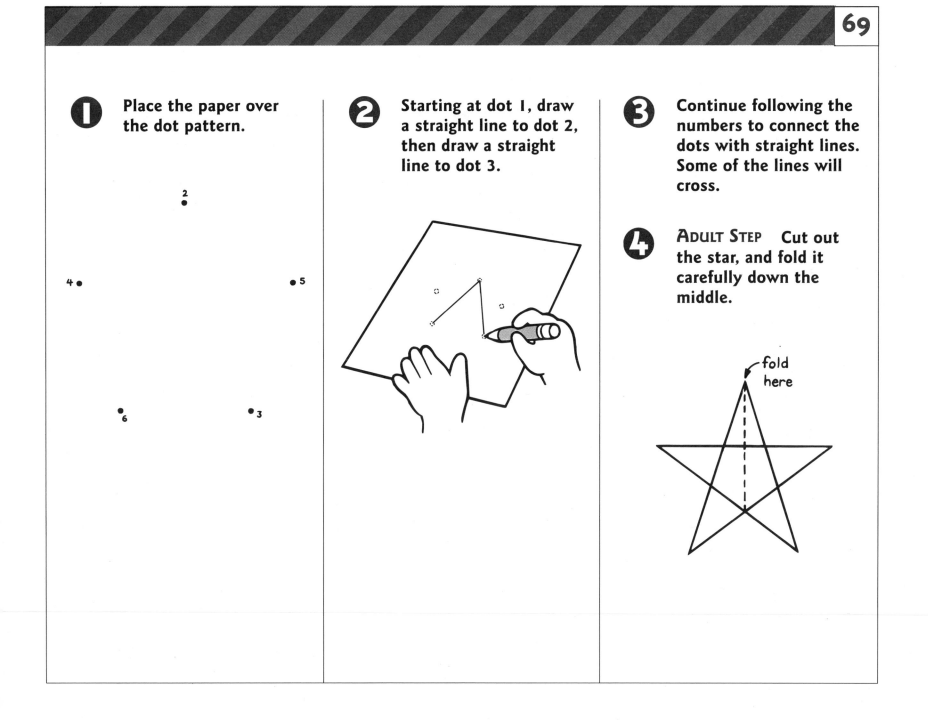

fold here

So Now We Know

You have made a five-pointed star. The five arms of the star design spread out from the center. Each arm is alike. When you fold your star down the middle, the right and left sides will match up exactly.

More Fun Things to Know and Do

You can make a star decoration.

- ADULT STEP   Use the cutting board and knife to cut a slice from the middle of the apple.

- Notice the five-pointed star design in the center of the slice.

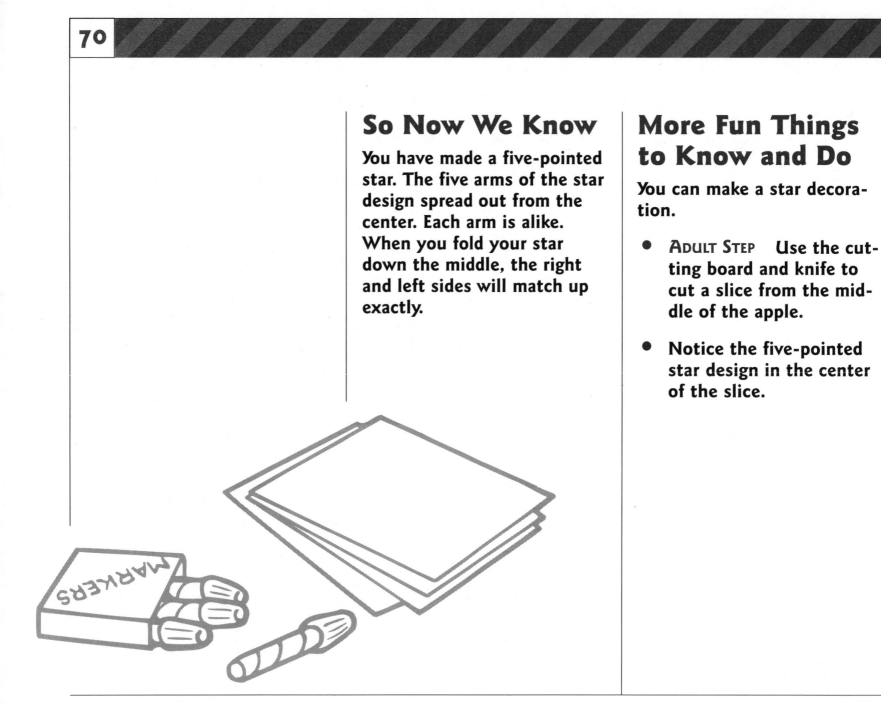

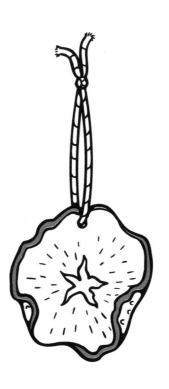

- When dry, hang the star in your room.

- Use the straw to make a hole near the edge of the slice.

- Tie the yarn through the hole and hang the slice where it can dry. It will take 2 to 3 days to dry.

Patterns

Linked

Round Up These Things

2 sheets of construction
  paper: I red, I white
scissors
transparent tape

Later You'll Need

4-by-8-inch piece of white
  paper
pencil
scissors
crayons

I wonder . . . How can I make a necklace?

Let's find out!

1 Fold each sheet of construction paper in half three times.

2 Unfold the papers and cut along all of the fold lines. You will end up with 16 strips: 8 red and 8 white.

3 Take a red strip and join the ends together with tape.

Take a white strip, run it through the red loop, and tape its ends together.

 Repeat step 4, adding a red strip and then a white strip, until all but one strip is used.

6 Run the last strip through the loops in both ends of the chain. Then, tape the ends of the strip together. The chain can be worn as a necklace.

So Now We Know

A chain is a number of loops joined together. Each loop in the chain is called a link. The paper-chain necklace that you made has links of two different colors, red and white, one after the other. This made a repeating pattern of red-white-red-white.

More Fun Things to Know and Do

Here's how you can make a repeating pattern of paper dolls.

- Fold the paper in half three times in the same direction.

- Unfold the paper and refold it along the fold lines so that it makes an accordion shape as shown.

- Draw the dashed pattern on one side of the folded paper as shown. Be sure that the folded and open edges of the paper are in the right place.

- ADULT STEP Cut the folded paper along the dashed lines.

- Unfold the paper and use crayons to draw faces, hair, and clothes on the paper dolls. Maybe you'd like to make a boy-girl pattern with your paper-doll chain.

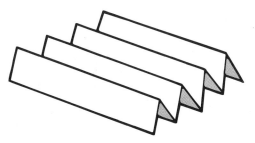

open edge →

fold

Repeating

Let's find out!

I wonder . . . How can I make a design?

Round Up These Things

cotton ball
liquid cooking oil
any shape cake pan (An older
  pan or a Teflon pan with a
  dark inside bottom works
  best.)
1 teaspoon (5 ml) flour
pencil

Later You'll Need

8-inch (20-cm) circle of white
  paper
scissors
pencil
12-inch (30-cm) piece of
  string

1 Wet the cotton ball with the oil.

2 Rub the wet cotton ball over the inside bottom of the pan so that the bottom of the pan is covered with a thin layer of oil.

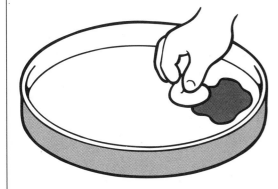

3 Put the flour in the pan.

4 Shake the pan back and forth to spread a thin layer of flour over the bottom of the pan. Shake the extra flour to one side by tilting the pan.

5 Use the pencil to draw a square in the flour. Place the square just above the center of the pan and to the left.

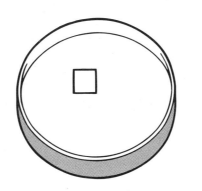

6 Draw two lines across the square from corner to corner to make an X. Now you have a square with four triangles inside.

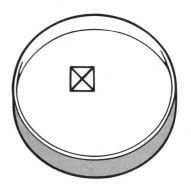

7 To the right of the square, draw another square that shares one side of the original square. Also draw an X in this square. Now you can see a diamond shape where the two squares join.

Below the two squares, draw two more squares with Xs. Now you can see a large diamond shape in the middle of a larger square. Can you also see the four big triangles pointing to the center?

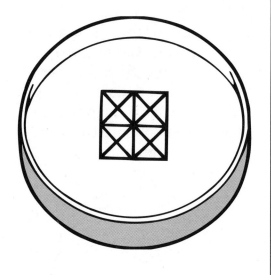

 Erase the design by shaking the pan back and forth to spread the extra flour over the design.

10 Try making more designs in the flour.

So Now We Know

Using just a few simple shapes, you were able to make many different designs. The designs were in repeating patterns.

More Fun Things to Know and Do

Use a repeating pattern to make a snowflake out of paper.

- Fold the paper circle in half.

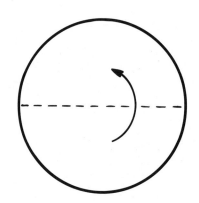

- **With the folded edge of the paper on the bottom, fold corner A to point B and corner C to point D as shown. (Points B and D are one-third of the way in along the curved edge from the corners.)**

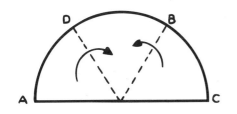

- **Fold the paper in half once more.**

- **ADULT STEP Cut off part of the folded paper as shown.**

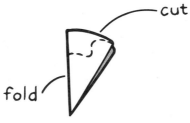

- **Draw triangles along the edges of the paper.**

- **ADULT STEP Cut out the triangles.**

- **Unfold the paper.**

- **Tie the string through one of the holes near the edge, and hang the paper snowflake in your room.**

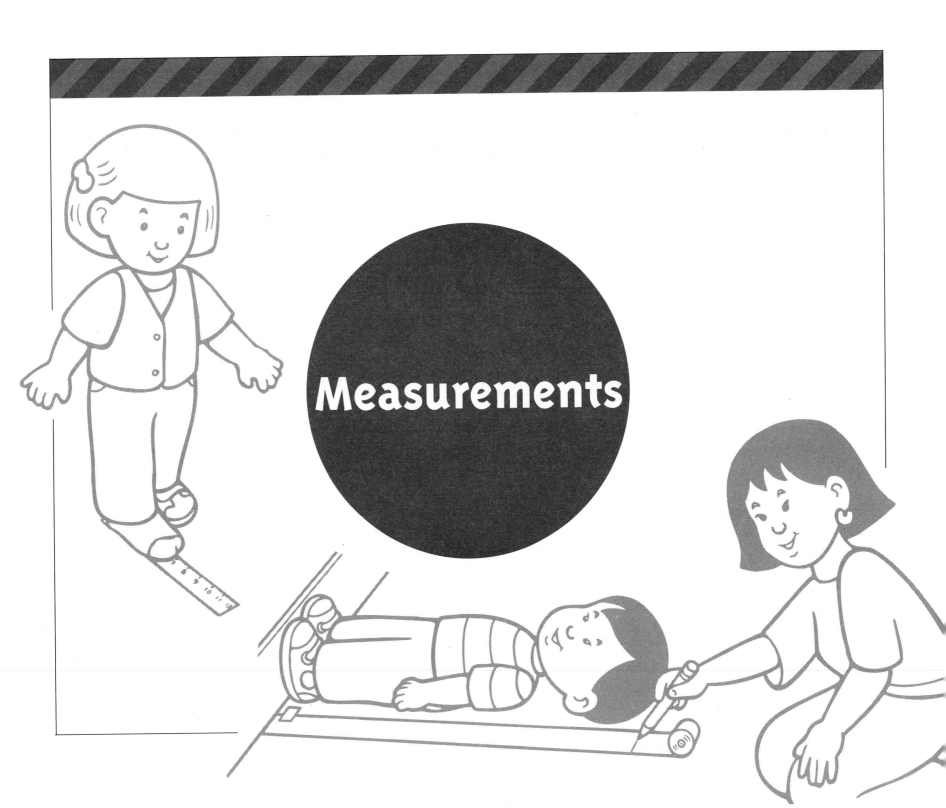

Measurements

Measure Up

1 Unroll about 12 inches (30 cm) of the adding-machine paper, and lay the roll on the floor so that the end of the paper touches a wall.

2 Secure the end of the paper to the floor with masking tape.

3 Lie on the floor next to the paper with your feet against the wall.

4 **ADULT STEP** Unroll more of the paper so that it is longer than the child's body. With the pencil, make a mark across the paper even with the top of the child's head.

5 Cut across the paper where it is marked, and tape this end of the paper strip to the floor.

6 Lay the measuring stick next to the paper strip so that the beginning of the stick is against the wall.

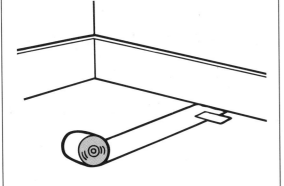

7 If the paper strip is longer than the measuring stick, make a mark on the paper at the end of the stick. The length of the stick is 36 inches (100 cm). Write this number next to the mark.

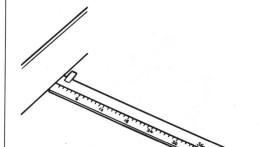

 8 Move the measuring stick so that the beginning is even with the mark. On the paper strip, write down the number closest to where the end of the paper touches the stick.

 9 Find your height by adding the two numbers together. On the paper strip shown, the length of the paper is recorded in inches. The height would be 36 + 12 = 48 inches.

10 Keep the paper strip for the next experiment.

So Now We Know

You have measured your height.

More Fun Things to Know and Do

For some people, the length of their outstretched arms is the same as or close to their height. See if this is true for you.

- Hold one end of the paper strip in each hand.

- As you hold the paper, stretch your arms outward. Is the paper long enough for you to completely outstretch your arms? Is the paper longer than your outstretched arms?

Royal Feet

Round Up These Things

12-inch (30-cm) ruler
your feet

Later You'll Need

1 or 2 helpers

1 Lay the ruler on the floor.

2 Take your right shoe off. Stand with your right heel at the beginning of the ruler. Does your foot reach all the way to the end of the ruler?

So Now We Know

On a ruler, 1 foot is equal to 12 inches (30 cm). This measure is called a foot because, in olden days, the length of the king's foot was used to measure things. Your foot is probably not a foot long, but some people have a foot that is as long as a ruler.

More Fun Things to Know and Do

Let's see how different the length of a room might be when different "royal feet" are used to measure it.

1 First, choose a royal person. (If you want, you can make him a crown from the "How Big" activity on page 92.) Give the royal person these instructions.

- Remove your shoes and socks.

- Stand with the heel of one foot against the wall, and place the heel of your other foot against your toes. This length is 2 royal feet from the wall.

←— 2 royal feet —→

- Lift the back foot and place its heel against the toes of the other foot. This length is 3 royal feet from the wall.

- Continue to move in a straight line across the room, counting each royal foot. Count the last royal foot only if it is at least half the length of your foot.

2 Select another royal person and have her repeat the previous procedure. Compare the room measurements made by the different royal feet. Are the lengths of the room the same?

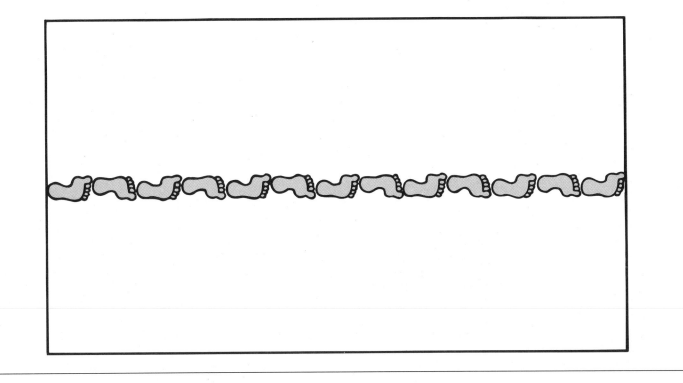

How Big?

Round Up These Things

24-inch (60-cm) strip of
  adding-machine paper
pencil
ruler

Later You'll Need

paper strip from original
  experiment
            plus
6-by-12-inch (15-by-30-cm)
  piece of yellow construction paper
pencil
scissors
transparent tape
school glue
glitter

1 Wrap the paper strip around your head across your forehead so that the ends of the paper overlap.

2 Holding the overlapping ends together, remove the paper strip from your head.

3 Use the pencil to make a mark where the ends of the paper overlap.

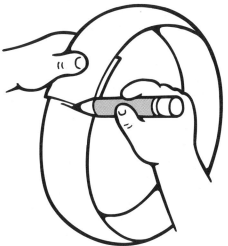

4 Lay the paper strip flat on a table. Use the ruler to measure the length of the strip from the end to the mark. This is how big around your head is. (Keep the paper strip for the next experiment.)

⑤ Repeat steps 1 through 4 to measure someone else's head. How does it compare to your head?

So Now We Know

You measured the distance around your head and around someone else's head. Then you compared the 2 measurements.

More Fun Things to Know and Do

Here's a way to make a crown that fits your head just right.

- Fold the piece of construction paper in half with the short ends together.

- Draw a design on the paper similar to the one shown.

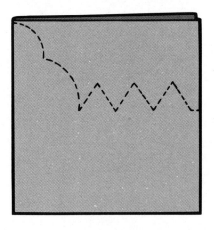

- **ADULT STEP** Cut out the design, cutting through both layers of paper.

- Lay the design on the paper strip made in the original experiment. Tape the design to the paper strip.

- Add jewels to the crown by placing dots of glue on the design and covering the glue with glitter.

- Tape the ends of the paper strip together at the mark you made.

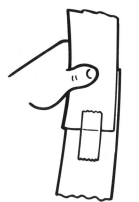

- Place the crown on your head. The crown is just your size.

Heavy

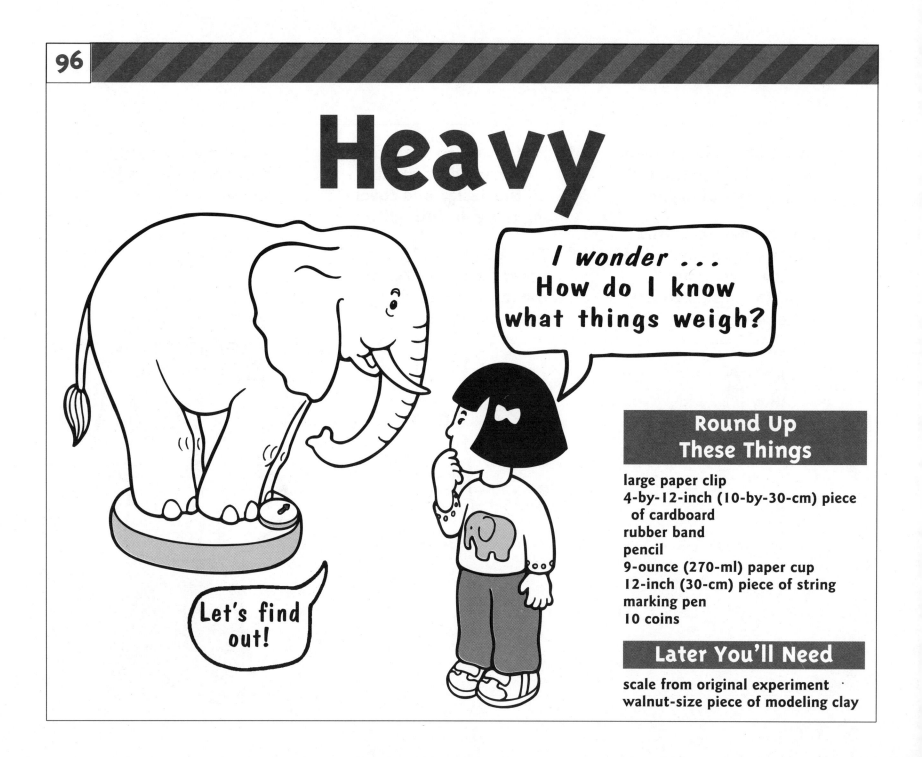

*I wonder ...
How do I know
what things weigh?*

Let's find out!

Round Up These Things

large paper clip
4-by-12-inch (10-by-30-cm) piece
  of cardboard
rubber band
pencil
9-ounce (270-ml) paper cup
12-inch (30-cm) piece of string
marking pen
10 coins

Later You'll Need

scale from original experiment
walnut-size piece of modeling clay

1 Attach the paper clip to the center of one of the short ends of the cardboard.

2 Hang the rubber band on the paper clip.

3 ADULT STEP   Use the pencil to punch two holes on opposite sides of the cup just under the rim.

4 Loop the string through the rubber band and tie the ends through each hole in the cup.

5 Hold the cardboard so that the cup hangs freely.

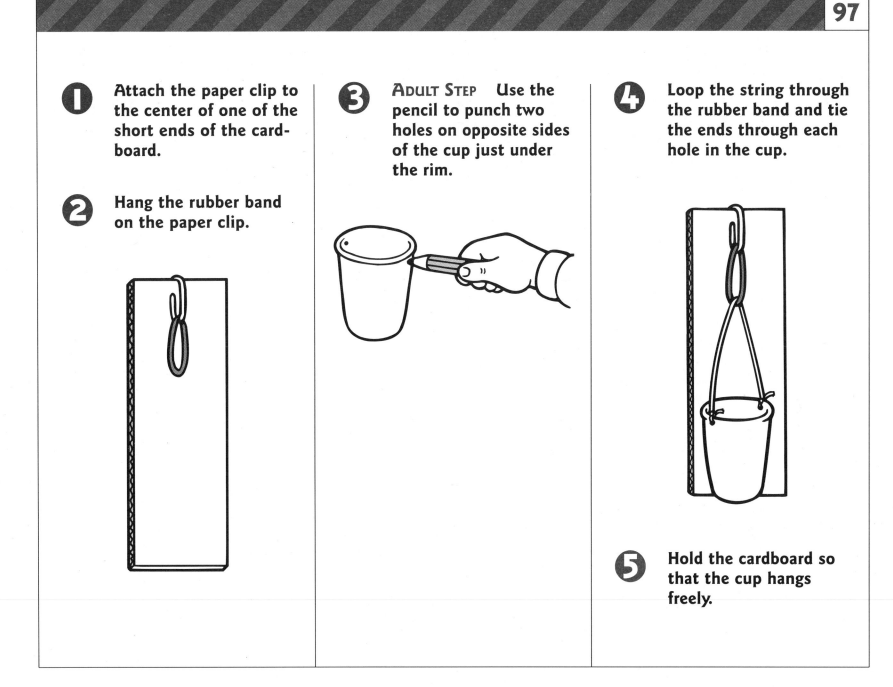

Use the pen to make a mark on the cardboard next to the bottom of the rubber band. You have made a scale.

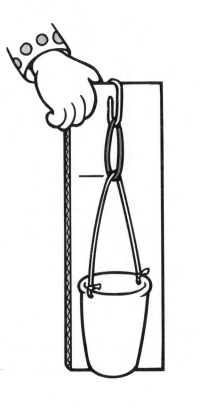

 Add 5 coins to the cup, and again mark the cardboard next to the bottom of the rubber band.

8 Repeat step 7, adding 5 more coins to the cup.

So Now We Know

Weight is a measure of how much something is pulled toward the earth. You know that 10 coins have more weight than 5 coins, because the cup was pulled down more.

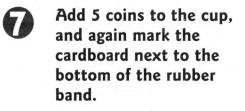

More Fun Things to Know and Do

Use your scale to compare the weight of other things to the weight of the coins.

- Use the clay to make a small figure of an animal that will fit inside the cup.

- Place the figure in the cup. Is the figure heavier than 5 coins? Than 10 coins?

Quantities

Covered

I wonder . . . How big is a leaf?

Let's find out!

Round Up These Things

8-inch (20-cm) square of white paper
ruler
pen
photocopier
5 to 10 sheets of newspaper
large leaf
green crayon

Later You'll Need

the same materials
plus
5 leaves with different shapes and sizes

1 Fold the white paper square in half three times from top to bottom.

2 Unfold the paper and fold it in half three times from side to side.

3 Unfold the paper and use the ruler and pen to draw lines across each of the fold lines to make 64 squares. You have made a sheet of graph paper.

4 Use a photocopier to make 4 copies of your graph paper. Save the original to use another time.

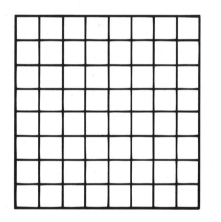

5 Stack the sheets of newspaper on top of each other.

6 Place the leaf, vein side up, on top of the stacked sheets of newspaper.

7 Cover the leaf with one of the copies of graph paper.

8 Rub the side of the crayon back and forth across the graph paper above the leaf. You will see a colored print of the leaf appear on the paper.

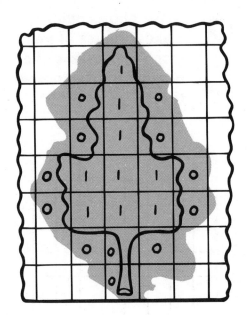

9 Look at the print of the leaf. Write a 1 in each square that is more than half covered by part of the leaf print. Write a 0 in each square that is less than half covered by the leaf print.

10 Count each square that has a number 1 in it.

So Now We Know

The size of a leaf is called its area. You found the area of your leaf by adding up the number of 1-inch squares it covers. The area of the leaf in the diagram is about 9 square inches.

More Fun Things to Know and Do

To estimate means to make a good guess. How good are you at estimating the area of things?

- Use the 5 leaves you picked.

- Look at the 5 leaves.

- Estimate the areas of the leaves, and lay them in order from the largest area to the smallest area.

- Use the graph paper and the procedure in the original activity to compare the areas of the leaves more accurately.

Was your estimate of the leaves' areas correct?

On the Mark

I wonder . . . How much soda is in my soda can?

Let's find out!

Round Up These Things

12-ounce (355-ml) can of soda
2-cup (500-ml) measuring cup

Later You'll Need

measuring cup
flour
2-quart (2-liter) bowl
salt
spoon
tap water
resealable plastic bag
cookie sheet
drinking straw
oven mitts
paintbrush
acrylic paints
24-inch (60-cm) piece of colored yarn
NOTE: This experiment requires an oven.

Open the can and pour the soda into the measuring cup.

 Look at the side of the measuring cup marked in cups.

 Find the top of the liquid, and read the number that is closest to the top of the liquid.

 Turn the cup around and look at the side marked in metric.

Read the number that is closest to the top of the liquid.

So Now We Know

There is a little more than 1½ cups of soda in the can. In metric measurements, this is a little more than 350 ml. The exact amount is written on the can: 12 ounces (355 ml).

More Fun Things to Know and Do

Use a measuring cup to make some baker's clay with this recipe. Then use the clay to make beads for a necklace.

- Pour flour into the measuring cup to the 1-cup (250-ml) mark. Pour the flour into the bowl.

- Add salt to the cup to the ½-cup (125-ml) mark. Pour the salt into the bowl.

- Mix the flour and salt together.

- Fill the cup with water to the ⅓-cup (83-ml) mark.

- Mixing with your hands, add a small amount of water at a time to the flour-and-salt mixture. Add enough water to make a smooth dough. If the dough is crumbly, add more water. If the dough gets too wet, sprinkle it with flour and mix again. If you don't want to use the dough right away, store it in a resealable plastic bag until you're ready to use it.

- To make beads, squeeze the dough into grape-size balls.

- Put the beads on a cookie sheet.

- Use the straw to poke a hole all the way through each bead.

- **ADULT STEP** Bake the beads at 250° Fahrenheit (120°C) for about 1½ hours or until dry. Use oven mitts to remove the beads from the oven. *Note:* Depending on humidity, beads will air-dry in one to three days.

- When the beads are cool, paint them with acrylic paints. Allow the paint to dry, then string the beads on the yarn. Your clay bead necklace is ready to wear.

Poppers

Round Up These Things

1-cup (250-ml) measuring cup
popcorn kernels
paper lunch bag or popcorn popper
masking tape
microwave
2-quart (2-liter) bowl

Later You'll Need

muffin mix
bowl
spoon
muffin pan liners
muffin pan
oven mitts
NOTE: This experiment requires an oven.

1 Measure ¼ cup (63 ml) of popcorn kernels.

2 Pour the popcorn kernels into the bag or popcorn popper. (If using a popcorn popper, follow the popper's instructions and skip to step 6.)

3 Close the bag by folding over about 1 inch (2.5 cm) of the top edge. Secure with tape.

4 ADULT STEP Place the bag in a microwave and heat for 2 minutes.

5 Allow the bag to cool for 5 minutes, then remove it from the microwave and open. *CAUTION: Popcorn from the microwave can be very hot! Do wait a full 5 minutes to allow it to cool before opening.*

6 Measure the popcorn. Do this by filling the measuring cup with popcorn, then pouring the popcorn into the bowl. Continue measuring until all the popcorn has been poured. Add up the number of cups (ml) of popcorn.

So Now We Know

When popcorn kernels are heated, they get bigger. The kernels changed from taking up ¼ cup (63 ml) of space to taking up about 3 cups (750 ml) of space.

More Fun Things to Know and Do

Other foods expand when heated. Experiment with some tasty muffins.

- Follow the instructions on the muffin mix to make the batter, using the bowl and spoon.

- Place a liner in each cup of the muffin pan. Fill the liners one-half (½) full with batter.

- you have a window in your oven door, watch with the child how the muffins change as they bake.

- After the muffins have cooled, look at the change in the size of the muffins. Compare the baked muffin with the uncooked batter in the liner. The batter fills one-half of the liner. How much space do the baked muffins take up?

- Fill an extra liner one-half full with batter and set it aside.

- ADULT STEP   Follow the instructions on the mix to bake the muffins. If

- ADULT STEP   Use the oven mitts to take the muffins out of the oven and set them aside to cool.

Recipe

**I wonder ...
How do I make a
peanut butter and
jelly sandwich?**

**Let's find
out!**

Round Up These Things

4 slices of bread
2 plates
1-tablespoon (15-ml) measuring spoon
peanut butter
dinner knife
paper towel
jelly
index card
scissors
pen
four 3-ounce (90-ml) paper cups
tap water
3 helpers

Later You'll Need

recipe card or index card
pen

1 Place 2 slices of bread on a plate.

2 Scoop 1 tablespoon (15 ml) of peanut butter out of the jar. Move the straight edge of the knife across the top of the spoon to remove any excess peanut butter. There should not be any peanut butter heaped above the spoon.

3 Use the knife to scrape all of the peanut butter from the spoon to one slice of bread and spread it around.

4 Wipe the knife and spoon clean with the paper towel.

5 Repeat steps 2 and 3 with the jelly and the second slice of bread.

6 Put the 2 slices of bread together with the peanut butter and jelly in the middle to make a sandwich.

7 Use the knife to cut the sandwich into 4 pieces.

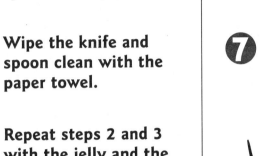

8 Repeat steps 1 through 7 to make another sandwich, but this time use 2 tablespoons (30 ml) each of peanut butter and jelly.

 9 Fold the index card in half with the short ends together. Unfold the card and cut it apart along the fold.

 10 Fold each piece of the card in half to make 2 stand-up cards. Write A on one of the cards and B on the other.

 11 Place the A card on the plate with the first sandwich and the B card on the plate with the second sandwich.

 12 Serve one of the sandwich pieces from plate A to each of your helpers and eat one piece yourself.

 13 After eating the sandwich pieces, you and your helpers should drink some water to wash out the taste of the sandwich.

 14 Repeat step 12 using the sandwich on plate B.

 15 Use your own opinion about the sandwich and those of your helpers to decide which sandwich tastes better.

So Now We Know

Cooks use special spoons to measure the ingredients in a recipe. Each spoon measures an exact amount so the recipe always comes out the same.

More Fun Things to Know and Do

Once you have decided on the amounts of peanut butter and jelly needed to make the perfect peanut butter and jelly sandwich, write out a recipe so you will always remember it. Here's an example of a written recipe.

Recipe for   A Peanut Butter and Jelly Sandwich

From the kitchen of Lacey Russell

Ingredients and Supplies:

1 dinner knife

2 slices of bread

2 tablespoons of peanut butter

2 tablespoons of jelly

- Spread the peanut butter on one slice of bread.
- Spread the jelly on the other slice of bread.
- Put the 2 slices of bread together.
- Cut the sandwich in half.

Appendix
Section Summaries

Counting

Counting is a basic math skill. "Petals" (pages 6–9) encourages children to count the petals of different kinds of flowers.

In "How Many?" (pages 10–13), children learn that one **dozen** means 12 things. Using an egg carton, children practice writing the numbers from 1 to 12 and counting out one dozen items. You may wish to use the carton to measure two dozen by placing two items in each egg cup. Counting by 2s, children will discover that two dozen means 24 things.

Addition and Subtraction

"Finger Math" (pages 16–19) shows how the fingers can be used to add and subtract numbers of five or less. You might explain that an **equation**, such as $2 + 3 = 5$, is a math sentence that reads two **plus** (add) three equals five. The equation for the subtraction prob-

lem five **minus** (take away) two is written: $5 - 2 = 3$.

In "Dinosaur Math" (pages 20–23), plastic figures are used to arrive at the answers to subtraction and addition equations. Another fun way to subtract would be to remove and eat a certain number of food pieces, such as dry cereal. Then, count the remaining pieces.

Fractions

A **fraction** is a number that represents part of a whole or group. When an object is cut into two equal parts, each part is half of the whole. The fraction for each part is written as ½. To cut an object in half, a straight line must be made across and through the center of the object. **Estimating** is making an educated guess about how much, how big, or how many. In "Just Alike" (pages 24–27), children first estimate the center of a solid, then cut it in half. A liquid is divided in half by comparing

the levels of the liquid in two identical containers.

In "Divided" (pages 28–31), fractional parts are first estimated by eye. Then, a slightly more accurate measuring technique, using a folded strip of paper, is used to find one-half (½) and one-fourth (¼).

Time

The amount of time equal to 5 seconds is measured in "Ticktock" (pages 34–37). Children discover that 5 seconds pass while the second hand moves from one number to the next on a clock. Counting by 5s, children discover that there are 60 seconds in 1 minute.

In "Day by Day" (pages 38–41), children use their hands to figure out the number of days in each month of the year. They also make a calendar and learn that a **leap year** has 366 days. Another way of remembering the days of the months is by reciting this poem:

Thirty days has September
April, June, and November
All the rest have thirty-one
When February's done
It's had twenty-eight days clear
And twenty-nine in each leap year

Forms

A **plane figure** is a two-dimensional geometric shape, such as a circle, oval, rectangle, square, triangle, or diamond. "Around and Around" (pages 44–47) shows children how to make a drawing tool and use it to draw a circle. A **circle** is a closed figure consisting of a line drawn around a real or imaginary center point. (A **closed figure** is a plane figure that begins and ends at the same point.) On a circle, each point on the line is the same distance from the center point. The children's drawing tool relies on the fact that a circle's **radius** is the distance from the center of the circle to any point on the line forming the circle. The distance between the holes on the tool is equal to the circle's radius. The **diameter** is the distance across the circle through its center point.

In "Magic or Math?" (pages 48–51), a math trick is used to demonstrate the difference between an oval and a circle. An **oval** is a closed figure that has an egglike shape, but the ends are equal in size. The ends of an oval are farther from the center point than the sides are. The **perimeter** (the distance around the outside of a closed figure) of each figure in the experiment is the same, but the oval is wider than the circle.

In "Three-Sided" (pages 52–55), children experiment with triangles to make a banner and a necklace. A **triangle** is a three-sided **polygon** (a closed figure formed by three or more lines that are joined only at their ends). The bead activity demonstrates the difference between **two-dimensional figures** (shapes or forms with length and width, such as drawings of rectangles, triangles, or circles), and **three-dimensional figures** (shapes or forms with length, width, and depth, such as beads).

In "Holders" (pages 56–59), children learn how to make two 3-dimensional forms, a box and a paper cup.

Symmetry

A **symmetrical figure** is one in which two halves mirror each other along a specific line through the figure. This line is called a **line of symmetry**. A figure that has two parts that mirror each other is said to have **bilateral symmetry**. "From the Heart" (pages 60–63) demonstrates bilateral symmetry with a valentine and a flower.

"Reversed" (pages 64–67) also shows bilateral symmetry. Children make paint-blot butterflies and learn an easy way to write their names backward.

Another type of symmetry is called radial symmetry. **Radial symmetry** means that the parts of the pattern spread out regularly from the center like the spokes of a wheel. "Star Designs" (pages 68–71) shows the radial symmetry of a five-pointed star.

Patterns

A **pattern** is a model or guide for something to be made from. It can also be a **design** and have a special arrangement or predictable sequence of things, such as shapes. The shapes may vary in size, color, or position, but they work together to form a pattern that can be recognized and extended. In "Linked" (pages 74–77), children create patterns by using colored paper to make a paper-chain necklace, and crayons and white paper to make a paper-doll chain. Shapes are often repeated to create patterns, such as patterns on ceramic floors and wall tiles. In "Repeating" (pages 78–81), children use repeating shapes of geometric figures to create patterns in flour and to make a paper snowflake.

Length

A ruler is used to measure length in both inches and centimeters. In "Measure Up" (pages 84–87), children measure their height, then compare their height to the length of their outstretched arms.

"Royal Feet" (pages 88–91) compares the length of the human foot to 12 inches. The English measuring system was originally based on human measurements, such as the length of a foot. A foot was the length of the king's foot, and a yard was the distance from the king's nose to the end of his thumb on his outstretched arm. Since the king was not always available, each person used his or her foot and outstretched arm to measure a foot or a yard. Differences in the size of human bodies led to the need for a more standard way of measuring. Thus, measuring tools such as the ruler were developed and are still used.

Circumference

The perimeter of a circle is called its **circumference**. While the human head is not perfectly round, the distance around it is called its circumference. In "How Big?" (pages 92–95), children measure the circumference of their heads and make crowns that fit just right.

Weight

A force called **gravity** pulls everything toward the earth. The amount of this force is called **weight**. Weight is measured in units called pounds (kg). "Heavy" (pages 96–99) demonstrates how a basic scale works. Home scales used to measure food or body weight can be used to further compare the weight of different objects.

Area

The amount of surface covered by a plane figure is called its **area**. On graph paper, the area of an object is the number of squares covered by the object. Since the squares on different graph papers vary in size, the area is expressed as the product of the number of squares covered times the area of each square. In "Covered" (pages 102–105), children make their own graph paper to estimate the area covered by leaves. The graph-paper squares are 1-inch square. Thus, the area of the leaf in the diagram is 9 square inches, which is calculated by multiplying: 9×1 square inch = 9 square inches.

Volume

A material's **volume** is how much space it takes up. "On the Mark" (pages 106–109) teaches children how to use a cup to measure volume. In rough comparisons between the English and metric systems, 1 cup is equivalent to 250 ml. A closer look at the markings on a metric cup will show that 1 cup is more equivalent to 237 ml. The experiment uses a can of soda to show that 12 ounces is equivalent to 355 ml. Children also measure quantities of flour, salt, and water to make baker's clay.

In "Poppers" (pages 110–113), children measure the change in volume of popcorn kernels before and after popping. The kernels expand and pop because tiny drops of water inside each kernel get hot and change into gas. This gas pushes out on the kernels, causing them to explode. In "The Recipe" (pages 114–117), children learn to measure volume with tablespoons.

Glossary

area The amount of surface covered by a plane figure.

bilateral symmetry The property of having a line of symmetry.

circle A closed figure consisting of a line drawn around a real or imaginary center point, with each point on the line being the same distance from the center point.

circumference The perimeter of a circle.

closed figures Plane figures that begin and end at the same point.

design A special arrangement or predictable sequence of things, such as shapes.

diameter The distance across a circle through its center point.

dozen A group of 12 things.

equation A math sentence that uses symbols, such as plus (+) or minus (–) and equals (=).

estimating Making an educated guess about how much, how big, or how many.

fraction A number that represents part of a whole or group.

gravity The force that pulls everything toward the center of the earth.

leap year A year with 366 days.

line of symmetry A line that divides a symmetrical figure into two halves that mirror each other.

minus Symbol (–) meaning to take away or subtract.

oval An egglike shape having ends that are equal in size and farther from the center point than the sides are.

pattern A model or guide for something to be made; an arrangement of parts; a design.

perimeter The distance around the outside of a closed figure.

plane figure A two-dimensional geometric shape, such as a circle, ellipse, rectangle, square, triangle, or diamond.

plus Symbol (+) meaning to add together.

polygon A closed figure formed by three or more lines that are joined only at their ends.

radial symmetry The property of having the parts of a design regularly spread out from the center like the spokes of a wheel.

radius The distance from the center of a circle to any point on the line forming the circle.

symmetrical figure A figure in which two halves mirror each other along a line of symmetry.

three-dimensional figures Shapes or forms with length, width, and depth, such as beads.

triangle A three-sided polygon.

two-dimensional figures Shapes or forms with length and width, such as drawings of rectangles, triangles, or circles.

volume The amount of space a material takes up.

weight A measure of how much an object is pulled toward the earth by gravity.

Index